As a first generation English medium learner, I owe this book to:

My Mother whose intellect, strength, and grit have inspired me to dare write these lines down;

My Guruji who allowed me a place in his life and taught me the worth of words; I owe it to him;

Bijit, for the endless inspiration through all these years;

And lastly, all the encounters, and characters who have left their silent yet lasting impression on my mind to make me a storyteller.

THE TALE OF A TOMORROW HOURGLASS

TOLD THROUGH 25 POEMS

ANKITA MANNA

Contents

Contents

Preface

An hourglass doesn't tell the time. It is merely a witness, silently watching the grains of sand tumbling away into a mirage they call an oasis. As they rush towards the other bulb and long for a place to settle down, the hourglass turns upside down.

But the hourglass never controls the flow of time. It doesn't discriminate. Never plugging the flow of good and bad memories, it merely watches on as a silent observer, stuck in a quandary of half-full and half-empty wishes.

These poems were written at different places and times in life, mainly during my adult life as an outsider, while I travelled across cities for academic and professional pursuits. Each one of them is deeply personal, with muddled-up thoughts from the days of childhood as they were narrated to me by elders I have eventually grown to call my family.

The constant search for a home and the indefinite futility of my search is what I have tried to capture through all these poems - either through people or places.

Looking back, it appears to me as episodic memories that unfold themselves while I encounter similar incidents as I move on in life.

Just like the sands that never settle, I continue my long journey for a hopeful "tomorrow". Even if the hourglass turns, I shall keep looking for my oasis - a place I can call home.

Acknowledgements

This book would not have been possible without Bijit and the team of The Tale of You and Notion Press. To those few friends who have stood by, listening to my rants and holding me when everything looked bleak. You know who you all are and I am grateful for you. My parents, for allowing me to live my life in my own terms, and understanding me, even when I could not understand myself. Thank you for your enormous trust in me. I will be nothing without you both.

1. To Ismail Chacha

I remember Ismail Chacha, who had the warmest smile and the kindest look
that he would flash at the students passing by.
He would carefully take the measurement of each student of our school that mounted
adjacent to his shop. He would often be called
the official dressmaker of our Christian Missionary School, though his surname would
often confuse people.

After graduating each class, we would get to enter Ismail Chacha's shop with our
parents who would often complain about the result that we would have had received a
while back, while Chacha would smile and say, "Don't worry, Beta. Next year you
will do better in Maths!"

I could never know how much Maths he knew himself, but he ensured to
accommodate our decimals that came along with each whole number. He would take
pride and say, "Beta, you are not 32, neither you are 34; you

are 33.3708" which only meant that his box was warm enough to give a shape to my uneven body.

And it is not just me; he would have room for every child who was a misfit and did not have a standard size. You see? Ismail Chacha was our genie who would give us hope at the end of each year to do better in the monotonous drudgery that now had a different class and section.

I don't know where he is now, probably in his shop where no one feels the need to go anymore?

I don't know if he still retains his smile or has himself been boxed into a category and size for his frail body, skin and colour.

Chacha would always promise us that those new uniforms would fit us exact, and they did. But now, it only lacked the smell of his hands.

2. The Boy

I used to wonder what poetry would look like until I met him, his uncanny eccentric natural habitat: his home. And here's the thing. The boy who feels like sunshine, and makes home wherever he is. He doesn't carry. He doesn't leave. He exists. Wherever he is. If only one engages long enough to understand the soothing voice while he hums some of Indian Ocean. A boy, nonchalant and yet so dignified; a man with so much integrity and a voice that stands out, even if it quivers in the face of the trouble, it is his voice nonetheless. He makes me wonder about the forest he carries within himself and what the woods would feel like on a wintry night while the wind ravages. He belongs there. To the mountains, to the stream flowing by, to the soil or the changing wind. He lives in all of them and yet none of them. He taps his desk with his feet, to match the rhythm of what he hums. The wood that connects him to the forest, perhaps. He sleeps peacefully next to me while I watch the

enormous possibilities
that he carries. Of being impregnated with the idea of being and living and
procreating, he reeks of it all. In the most uninhibited, rustic, animalistic self, he is the
most humane human I've ever seen.

3. View from a Hotel Room

The cars keep moving,
and then sparse, faster now;
the cold breeze brushes the cheeks,
hair ruffled, a little tired.
The train honks at a distance,
clamours from the rooms -
some still lit up,
some dark.
Friends cheer to drink, to new life;
another drink to please, while
the stranger heaves, still trying to adjust
to the rubber that's stuck, displeased.
The lights glitter, the city sleeps,
yet awake, in its own right.
Through the bylanes, the cow dung ferments.
The drains still reek
of nights gone by,
and the nights to come,
and the night that is -
he will be remembered.

4. Abyss

Where do you even begin to search when all you know you have is an abyss? And
then you adjust your eyes to start seeing darkness illumine. They all tell you it is going
to be okay, and you know it too, but how do you control this sinking feeling when you
know all you're left with is a ship, with its mast broken and compass long lost?

Moreover, you know that probably the journey would look bleaker had there been
a compass in the first place.

How do you tame a heart that has always found home in all the odd places?

And then you question after a while: when did you hear the piano stop playing?
While you kept looking at the spider webbing around the broken leaf,
just about hanging, and calling it its home? You wonder if you've been home all this
while, and then ask if all you needed was someone to tell you

that you have been
home all this while, you stupid heart. You hear all the mutterings, from the bedlam
beside and the brothel next to it. Both complaining. Of not having rested well enough.
And how the food was not good that day too. You sit there. You wonder. You see the
abyss, in all its glory,
of darkness illumine.

5. Him

Water droplets rolling down his body while his hands search for crevices one dare not
touch. She breathes heavy, clenching and kissing at the same time. His masculine
sinews finding solace in the caves of virgin beauty, slithering in ways she never could
imagine. He grabs her by the waist, her pulsating body revealing more than words.
Beads of sweat break and mingle with the water, not knowing where to find respite. So
they find each other, in exploration, desire and silence.

6. Mother

The mother calls for the auto,
frail hands gesturing to stop.
Gently, she holds her pregnant daughter,
lifting with all her might.
They bend with their load,
one with her dreams and
the other with the broken ones.

They ride.

The auto crosses traffic
with each speed breaker.
She touches her belly,
not knowing if she can truly protect him.
The mother caresses her hair.
Sweat beads break,
and with that, a little smile too -
of exhaustion and anticipation.
The auto stops, they get down;
unsteady steps towards the hospital gate,
feet with cracks that reek of life,
unkempt nails, faded and tousled.

7. First Day, Tomorrow

So here I am, back to square one, exactly where I had begun. But this time, with a
sense of loss to begin with. You see, not everything we gain is a gain, and not everything
we lose qualifies as a loss unless one knows in his heart what loss amounts to.

So here I am,
re-thinking,
re-reading in the process of learning and unlearning about myself. A process that has been
a discovery and a painful interaction every day,
a self that I have loathed and loved just the same.

While I have managed to drag myself out of bed every single day, I have also
managed to lose what was a part of me that was prematurely let go of. I wasn't ready.

Perhaps never will be either.

This has been a constant introspection, a process I have hated for the longest time.

They talk about friends, family, love, jealousy, and hatred - all of it which never made
any sense to me. It all boils down to me returning to that lonely room each night
although I have the entire apartment to myself.

Here's the thing, I perhaps have become accustomed to inflict it on myself, to magnify the sense
of loneliness by adding two more rooms adjacent to mine, only to emphasise that they're deserted.
I often ask myself the questions that I evade during moments of glory and eventually
end up loathing myself a little more: Did I know all of it all this while? Did I not step
into it knowing how it is bound to end? Did I not begin it in the first place knowing
that there is an end to it too? How do I even manage to continue to damage a self that
has known the scheme behind that damage? And who is really to be blamed when I
devise that scheme way too well? With all these thoughts pricking my conscience, I
manage to sleep every night. Tossed, turned, broken at times but sleep it is
nonetheless.

I have been told several things by too many people. Of all the things I've heard, "annoying" and "irritating" continue to remain my favourites. For someone to call me those reveals a certain sense of belongingness in the first place. I pleasure myself into believing that perhaps I've made my presence felt enough for the person to feel irritated by the non-pattern that I am capable of coming up with; it also shows a certain sense of habit. I am unsure if this is the voyeur in me speaking or simply the moron who is lonely and miserable. You see, I would like to believe that it is the voyeur because who likes to be identified as the miserable one? So yeah, here I am,

back to square one. Tomorrow is my first day. Wish me luck?

8. The Lover

How many lives do I have to live,
to understand Life in all its glory?
How many heartbreaks do I need
to undergo, to understand Love in all its misery?
I see Mother taking a last look at the photograph, before shelving it once again into her
old diary, a photograph that smiled back at her but she didn't.
The wrinkled pages with ink blots and lines that reek of termites and nostalgia,
the leather jacket pressed beyond limits.
Rims of the steel bowl have started to crack finally.
After all, how long do you want it to hold itself back?
I take a long pause before I take off the garland from the wooden frame;
notice it has developed mites too.
The wall has become undulated.
Whitewashing couldn't hide the stains of violence.
I walk past the corridor; it seemed like a drudgery to clean up the cobweb.
What right does one have to break someone's home?
The sun glares on top, the leaves dry up,
unable to withstand the brunt.
I smirk at the idea of a warm sun, sweating.

Before I let myself lie down, beneath the old tree,
the bark read, "Shehzad loves Priya."

9. Father

Did you do it to Mother too?
Beaten her black and blue,
and ask her frail body to graze the cattle and tame the black horse too?

10. To Baba

If Baba knew of it, he would know how much his daughter
felt hurt;
he would try with all his might
to protect that child in her;
the child who would often come to him,
and despite the shoulder pain,
Baba would lift her in his arms,
and make sure she never sheds a tear.
The world is cruel, Baba.
No one knows how to love like you;
no one would care to ask
when they see your daughter cry.
Baba, you should have prepared me harder
to face them every day,
the friends that feel like demons,
way too often.
Baba, when you are gone,
your little child will remember you as the
kindest man with the warmest heart;
she would be the man you were,
and face the world,
to make it a warmer and kinder place,
like you did, always.

11. I Remember the Last Time

I remember the last time I saw you,
leaving and fading into memories,
like those unknown railway stations
no one cares to remember,
like the flittering lights
on lonely winter nights,
while the cheap hotel rooms fume,
or the balloon-seller, after the fair.

I remember the last time I saw you,
withering smile as your silhouette disappeared,
like the poles we walk past,
lighting our ways, while we barely notice,
I remember you in all those silent nights
that often break into doleful mornings,
after the new bride leaves her home
for the unknown.

12. The Dream

We wondered looking at the stars,
what aeons ago the world must have looked like,
like the new-age Adam and Eve, waiting for their vice.
She pressed my hands gently,
before letting it be in hers forever.

The sand and the moon remained the only witnesses
to our culmination.
She let me rest my head on her lap,
embalming my pains and turning them to joy:
Was she a woman? A lover? Or a sage?
One never knows, until she disappeared into oblivion.
My eyes opened as I heard the water ripple,
untouched and immaculate by her absence.
Was she a dream? A sin? Or a fantasy?
Was she the figment of what they call an ecstasy?

13. Of Old Habits

How do you exactly tame a heart that has been frivolous all its life?
A man entering to fan the fire
of loins that have known what fluttering meant.
How does one deal with an ever-elusive lover?
To try and join the dot in every possible connection,
and the incessant urge to hold on to remnants of the past,
of rains that will only bring flood and not respite.
How does one justify the means of escape?
You see, we are traveling backward in Time,
recalculating and recalibrating each emotion,
as we accept the times impending.
When is one ever ready even when the Truth looms large?
When does one know what to do with an untamed heart?

14. Regular

Mother does not speak much.
The entire day she brooms, cleans, and mops.
Father doesn't look at her face anymore.
He does not recognize the wrinkles on her face.
Mother barely sits now; she prefers to lie down.
I listen to her whimper every night as she goes to bed.

15. Lust

He clenched his hands against mine, our skin rubbing against each other.
The sultry bodies intertwined into a mesh of chaos, trying to answer the questions in
silences.
As he pulled me closer, he looked into my eyes, still perspiring, hands finding ways
through the crevices, and said, "I am home."

16. Of Oblivion

Maybe people left for a reason.
Perhaps it was way too much -
two broken souls, trying relentlessly
to be understood.
Sun that had lost the charm,
Home that was almost broken,
The butterfly selling colours,
striving to make dreams come true.
It wasn't about forgiveness
or acceptance that had now lost count,
waiting to be misunderstood again.

Pills that were almost taken,
the loud noises in the head
that just wouldn't stop.
Half-baked romance of supposed culmination,
tiring days of carrying the hearse.
It's been so long since he smiled.
Weary roads that led to nothingness.
He became the monster she feared,
or was he always this way?
There was no living with him,
nor without him.

She couldn't stand who she'd become.
So how does one carry on?
Childhood that pained,
Warmth that was long forgotten,
They wished for a Home,
A Home that might never be.
But, what if it it worked?
Better to die with memories
than lonely blankets in oblivion.
What if the risk was already taken?

17. Of Transfers

It's been a long ride which took me to the city:
new signboards and strange letters.
The city seemed to be welcoming me
with the quirks and cries of the street hawkers.
The unfamiliar bed reminded me of home,
and all the things that the whitewashed walls lacked; it was stranger than the man in
the bus.
Once I unpacked, and figured out all that I'd missed, I discovered the familiar smell of
Mother's carefully packed pickle that refused to obey without spilling over.

18. One Day

When all this is over, let's go out for a walk,
you and I, away from the deafening noise.
I still hope that day will arrive
when we'd talk finally, in silence.

19. An Ode to Farewell

Even before we realize we have arrived,
it is time to leave.
What does one do when the centre keeps changing?
What truths do you hold on to?
How do you say goodbye when
you never arrived in the first place?
How does one deal with loss when
loss seems like the only gain?
A farewell, they say, is a goodbye.
But how does one know when it is the last time?
With a concept of Time that's constantly moving,
does our movement truly count?
In this mesh of Time and Truths,
may this be the beginning of many ends,
and may these ends open doors
for the many beginnings we look for.

20. Metamorphosis

Will you be the same if I tell you that I wasn't the person you were kissing last night?
Or the smell that you got from your mom's skin reeks of blood of someone else who's
dying?
Will you come to terms if I told you the man you just abused had lost his son last
morning?
Or the pizza delivery boy whom you tipped was on the verge of giving up?
Will you think of me the same way if I said I had lied to you the times I said I was
sleepy because I wanted to talk to someone else?
Will you hold me just the same if I said you weren't that man for me?
Will you let go of all the feelings that metamorphosed into what we called "our
world"?
Would you still believe in me if I said I need you?
Will you still trust the kid who stole and said it was for something he lacked?
Will you forgive the sinner who debauched himself into things he never wanted to be?

Will you believe me if I told you it's never too late yet and let's give it a shot?
Will you still give yourself a chance to not be off the grid?
Will you look at the sky with me and think of Time that showed us what we loved and
lost?
Or on rainy afternoons, will you hug me just the same knowing this skin doesn't
belong to us?

21. Of Longing

We would walk together for the longest time,
of the times when we promised each other
to lend a shoulder to cry on,
or hands to clasp onto.
We would cry together the nights that would be too unbearable,
whose weight would make us breathless,
and question our sheer existence or the fact we breathe,
and ask if we did all right at the end.

We would stand together against the mirror,
and fight the demons within us as we struggle to hold on nonetheless.
We would face the world as they label us into a box,
and try and throttle as we strive to speak up.
We would bask in the glory of the unknown crevices that we will discover in each
other,
of the stories long buried within,
of the desires that seeped deeper in,
of the guitar strings long broken.
We would hold the world we create in each other,
and smell heaven as they call it and embed time

with the miniscule insignificant capsule that would preserve our memories and beyond.
Perhaps, Time will remember us,
for our love and longing.

22. You Are Remembered

For the days which pass by,
without anything worth mentioning,
I want you to know that
even on those days, you're remembered.
Without reason or expectations,
like the sunrays on a broken column,
in an old dilapidated pillar,
often forgotten, but history remembers.
The mornings when you're absent-minded,
unaware of your path towards the end,
just the casual walks
reminding you of your existence.
The breeze that kisses your cheeks
without bothering you,
something that you've grown used to,
as an embrace which you never had felt.
Amidst all the agony of drudgery
and cacophony that often ends up silencing
your mind and gives voice to your soul,
you're remembered, in all those moments.

23. That Song

I heard that song again.
After all this time, I listened to it.
I can't lie that I didn't get reminded
of you, of us and your smell.
The memories that pained,
but not anymore.
It's funny how agony finds escape
through songs,
lyrics that speak on our behalf,
of things that we dare not speak out,
of things lost in longing,
of heartbreaks still clinging.

As I listen to that song again,
I remember you and how you
could walk away,
leaving nothing but wrinkled bed sheets
and me, both wanting to hold you back
a little longer.
I can't say I felt lonely.
Perhaps this is what music does to you.
You get used to being alone
with lyrics that give you company.

This time, tears didn't trickle.
It only proved that I was healing.
Do you too dare to listen to the same song?
Does it remind you of me
and the things undone?
Do you think it was just?

Well? Do you get away with
deceiving yourself at every face-off?
The rantings of the crooked mind
have finally found respite.
This song doesn't conspire anymore.
It only recalls but never triggers
thoughts that were long lost
under the weight of masks I wear.
The food gets delivered,
the song plays on
in a loop, creating a concoction
of prompts and promises
that were never spoken,
thoughts that were long forsaken.
I walked through the same lanes today.

For a change, I could face the sound
of the usual banters and words
of the familiar faces.
I walked today without expectations

of reciprocation.

24. That Night

And that night, he spoke in silence,
about the time when he was broken.
Words that were almost forgotten,
but memories that would still torment.
What is it that scared him?
Eyes that revealed he almost had them.
But alas, life was just a game,
gambling emotions to win over shame.
It isn't the words that hurt,
but the actions that still remain.
The nights of supposed culmination
leave him aching for warmth he'd never gotten.
That night, when she looked at him,
he spoke. He spoke of the darkest nights,
that pushed him harder to recoil,
something that left his heart in turmoil.
What did he hide behind that smile?
Faces that often beguiled.
Was it the love he never received?
Or the pain of trusting the ones that deceived?
The promises that were half-spoken,
now knew how to be strengthened.
And when she looked at him that night,

that night he spoke, through silence.

25. Bikhre

The ukulele chords play as we are introduced to a world that reminds us what lies within and beyond.

Bikhre is a love song that goes like a lullaby, trying to calm the heart of a forlorn lover, to haunt us in the most subtle way possible. It is a staunch reminder of how fragile and scary love truly is. To be able to trust someone with your life and feel the most powerful and most vulnerable at the same time. It is the strength we gather before taking that breath that we hold before kissing those lips and then letting it all go in a moment and forgetting the world around us as we exchange the energy. The hauntingly beautiful chords play on once we move to the realisation that it is perhaps too late to let go, or too early to feel frightened. It's the constant dilemma in the mind before the final confession to want to hold the hand. It is a reminder of those actions and words that we take notice of without letting the other person know and try to keep it as subtle to avoid being exposed.

Those nights spent on rewinding the entire day to arrive at those conversations, and replay them till the eyes feel tired. It's perhaps the voice, the beads of sweat, the puckered-up lips before the smile or simply, the rhythm of breathing that orchestrates to create this uncanny restlessness that overwhelms us. *Bikhre* reminds us of all the scattered ways in which the lover lives on, in moments of sleepless nights or helplessness. The inability to reach out, the fluttering heartbeats while re-reading the old texts and eventually trying to read in between those lines, to make sense of what it actually meant. *Bikhre* scatters us in the most wonderful way possible to remind us of the futility in trying to make sense of everything, only to make us realize that eventually, it was all for that feeling that transcended the person without us knowing it.

Bio

Ankita Manna, born and raised in erstwhile Calcutta, holds a master's degree in English Literature from Lady Shri Ram College, University of Delhi. She currently works as a communicator and content developer while trying to learn the tricks of the corporate world. When not working, she can be found playing with kids or listening to stories from strangers. She is intrigued by the complexities of behavioral psychology and human relationships. *The Tale of a Tomorrow Hourglass* is her first attempt to give shape to the draft that she had so long kept safe in her computer hard-drive.

9 798887 495552

Printed by Libri Plureos GmbH in Hamburg,
Germany